BIOGI
KATHLEEN GLASGOW

Illuminating the Human Experience
Through Words

Brown Ford

Copyright
All right reserved

TABLE OF CONTENT

INTRODUCTION

In the world of young adult literature, few authors possess the unique ability to reach deep into the hearts and minds of their readers quite like Kathleen Glasgow. Born on February 12, 1969, in the picturesque city of Tucson, Arizona, Kathleen's life story is a testament to the transformative power of words and the enduring impact of storytelling.

From her earliest days, Kathleen Glasgow was drawn to the magic of books. Growing up in the arid landscapes of Tucson, she found solace in the pages of novels, forging a connection with the characters and stories that transported her to far-off places and introduced her to a tapestry of emotions. Little did she know that this childhood passion would one day shape her destiny.

As Kathleen grew, so did her passion for the written word. She pursued her education at the University of Arizona, where she delved into the realm of English and creative writing. It was during these formative years that she began to sharpen her skills, crafting narratives that hinted at the talent that would one day captivate readers mind worldwide.

But Kathleen's journey into the literary world was no fairy tale. It was a path fraught with twists and turns, one that saw her venture into diverse writing-related roles, from copywriting to freelance journalism. These experiences, though not glamorous, provided invaluable insights into the art of writing and the inner workings of the publishing industry.

Then came the turning point. In 2016, Kathleen Glasgow released her debut novel, "Girl in Pieces." This singular work would become a literary phenomenon, an emotionally charged exploration of themes like self-harm and resilience. Through the eyes of her protagonist, Charlie Davis, Kathleen demonstrated her uncanny ability to delve into the darkest corners of the human experience and emerge with stories that resonated with authenticity.

Yet, Kathleen's journey didn't stop there. Her subsequent novels, including "How to Make Friends with the Dark" and "You'd Be Home Now," further cemented her status as a formidable talent in the realm of young adult literature.

But beyond the printed pages, Kathleen's personal journey is as riveting as any story she's penned.

Her candidness about her own battles with mental health and recovery has given her work a unique depth and poignancy, connecting with readers on a profoundly personal level.

As we embark on this biographical exploration, we'll delve into the life, influences, and creative spirit of Kathleen Glasgow. We'll unveil the woman behind the words, the author whose storytelling prowess has touched countless lives and continues to shape the landscape of young adult literature. So, join us on this literary journey as we discover the remarkable story of Kathleen Glasgow.

EDUCATIONAL JOURNEY

Kathleen Glasgow's pursuit of her passion for literature and writing took her on an educational journey that played a pivotal role in shaping her as a writer. Her years at the University of Arizona were a transformative period, where she honed her skills and cultivated her creative talents.

At the University of Arizona, Kathleen embarked on a rigorous academic path with a focus on English and creative writing. These disciplines provided her with a structured framework to explore her love for words, stories, and the complexities of human expression.

Within the hallowed halls of academia, Kathleen encountered professors and mentors who recognized her potential and nurtured her burgeoning talent. Their guidance, feedback, and mentorship became invaluable assets in her growth as a writer. Under their tutelage, she refined her writing style, learned to dissect the nuances of storytelling, and gained a deeper appreciation for literature's power to illuminate the human experience.

Throughout her educational journey, Kathleen's dedication to her craft was evident. She immersed herself in a diverse array of literary genres, from classic literature to contemporary works. This wide-ranging exposure broadened her literary horizons, enabling her to draw inspiration from a rich tapestry of voices, narratives, and literary traditions.

As Kathleen Glasgow progressed through her academic years, she didn't just absorb knowledge; she actively engaged in the writing community.

She participated in writing workshops, collaborated with fellow aspiring authors, and even contributed to campus literary publications. These experiences provided her with practical, hands-on opportunities to apply her growing skills and receive constructive feedback.

It was during her time at university that Kathleen Glasgow began to develop her unique voice as a writer. She experimented with different writing techniques, genres, and themes, gradually molding her identity as an author. Her academic pursuits were not merely a means to an end but a genuine passion that she pursued with unwavering dedication.

This educational journey laid the foundation for Kathleen's future as a writer, equipping her with the literary prowess, critical thinking skills, and storytelling sensibilities that would define her as a prominent voice in the world of young adult literature. Little did she know that the lessons learned and the relationships forged during these formative years would play a pivotal role in her ascent as a celebrated author.

ENTRY INTO THE WRITING WORLD

Kathleen Glasgow's transition from a young, aspiring writer to a recognized author was a journey marked by determination, perseverance, and a touch of luck. Her early foray into the writing world was characterized by a series of diverse experiences that ultimately paved the way for her emergence as a literary talent.

After completing her studies at the University of Arizona, Kathleen embarked on her quest to make a mark in the world of words. Her first steps led her to explore various writing-related roles that would provide her with a practical understanding of the craft. She dabbled in copywriting, where she honed her ability to craft persuasive and engaging prose. This initial exposure to the world of marketing and communication sharpened her skills and introduced her to the power of words in different contexts.

While copywriting offered Kathleen a steady source of income, her true passion lay in creative writing. She ventured into freelance journalism, contributing her writing to various publications. This experience allowed her to exercise her creativity and versatility as a writer, covering a range of topics and engaging with different audiences.

Though these early roles may have seemed like stepping stones to some, for Kathleen, they were crucial in providing a foundation of practical experience. She gained insights into the art of storytelling, understanding how to captivate readers and convey ideas effectively.

It was during this period of exploration that Kathleen Glasgow's determination to pursue a career as an author began to solidify. She realized that her love for writing was not confined to a hobby but a calling she couldn't ignore. The stories she wanted to tell, the characters she wanted to breathe life into, and the themes she wanted to explore demanded a more profound and dedicated commitment.

With a growing body of work and a clearer vision of her literary aspirations, Kathleen took a leap of faith and made the bold decision to pursue her passion for creative writing wholeheartedly. This pivotal moment marked the true beginning of her journey as an author. She began to channel her energy and creativity into crafting stories that would resonate with readers on a profound level.

The path to becoming a published author was not without its challenges and uncertainties, but Kathleen's unwavering determination and the diverse experiences she had accumulated provided her with a solid foundation. Her entry into the writing world was not just a career choice; it was a lifelong dream unfolding, setting the stage for the literary achievements that would follow in the years to come.

DEBUT NOVEL – " GIRL IN PIECES"

The inspiration behind Kathleen Glasgow's novel "Girl in Pieces" is deeply rooted in her own experiences and a desire to shed light on important issues surrounding mental health and self-harm. Kathleen has been candid about her personal journey, including her struggles with mental health, which played a significant role in shaping the themes and narrative of the book.

"Girl in Pieces" is a poignant and emotionally charged young adult novel that delves deep into the life of the protagonist, Charlie Davis, as she navigates a harrowing journey of self-discovery, recovery, and resilience. The novel is a raw and unflinching exploration of the human capacity to endure pain and find healing in unexpected places.

Charlie Davis is a teenager who has known her fair share of suffering. Haunted by a traumatic past, she finds herself in a downward spiral of self-destructive behavior, marked by self-harm and an inability to cope with her emotional pain. After a series of traumatic events, including the loss of her best friend, Charlie ends up in a treatment center for girls struggling with similar issues.

Inside the facility, Charlie begins the difficult process of healing. She meets a cast of characters who have their own stories of pain and survival, forming deep connections with them as they confront their demons together. Through therapy sessions, art therapy, and the support of her newfound friends, Charlie slowly starts to piece herself back together.

One of the most striking aspects of "Girl in Pieces" is Kathleen Glasgow's ability to authentically portray Charlie's inner turmoil and the complexities of her emotions. The novel doesn't shy away from the difficult subject of self-harm but approaches it with compassion and empathy, shedding light on the experiences of those who struggle with it.

As Charlie progresses in her recovery, she begins to discover her talent for art and uses it as a means of expression and healing. Her journey toward self-acceptance is marked by setbacks and triumphs, and readers are taken on a rollercoaster ride of emotions as they witness her growth.

Throughout the novel, Glasgow tackles themes of mental health, self-identity, the power of friendship, and the importance of finding one's voice in the face of adversity. "Girl in Pieces" is a testament to the human spirit's resilience and the capacity for individuals to reclaim their lives and their sense of self, even in the darkest of times.

Kathleen Glasgow's debut novel is a powerful and compelling work that has resonated deeply with readers, earning critical acclaim for its honest portrayal of challenging subject matter and its message of hope and healing. It serves as a reminder that, even in the depths of despair, there is the potential for transformation and redemption.

THEMES AND IMPACTS

THEMES

Kathleen Glasgow's work explores a range of themes that resonate deeply with readers, often delving into complex and sensitive subjects. Here is an exploration of some recurring themes in her writing:

1. **Mental Health and Recovery**: One of the central and most prevalent themes in Kathleen Glasgow's work is mental health. Her novels often focus on characters who grapple with various mental health issues, including depression, anxiety, self-harm, and trauma. Through their experiences, Glasgow shines a light on the importance of acknowledging and addressing

mental health challenges. Her narratives underscore the journey of recovery and the resilience of the human spirit.

2. **Self-Discovery and Identity**: Kathleen's characters frequently undergo journeys of self-discovery and self-acceptance. They grapple with questions of identity, trying to find their place in the world and understand who they truly are. These themes of self-exploration resonate with young adult readers who are navigating the complexities of adolescence and coming into their own identities.

3. **Friendship and Support**: Friendship and the power of human connection are recurring themes in Glasgow's novels. Her characters often form deep and meaningful bonds with others who offer support and understanding during challenging

times. These friendships serve as sources of strength and comfort, highlighting the importance of a support system.

4. **Art and Creativity**: Art, in various forms, plays a significant role in many of Kathleen's stories. Whether it's painting, writing, or another creative outlet, art serves as a means of self-expression and healing for her characters. The act of creating art often helps them process their emotions and find a sense of purpose.

5. **Family Dynamics**: Family relationships are another dimension explored in Kathleen's work. Her novels depict both the complexities and the enduring bonds within families. She portrays the impact of family dynamics on her characters' lives, including the challenges and sources of strength that family can provide.

6. **Resilience and Hope**: In the face of adversity, Kathleen's characters display remarkable resilience. Her novels are imbued with a message of hope, emphasizing that even in the darkest moments, there is the potential for growth, recovery, and a brighter future.

7. **Realistic and Relatable Characters**: Kathleen Glasgow is known for creating realistic and relatable characters. Her protagonists often face relatable struggles, making them accessible to readers who may see themselves in the challenges these characters confront. This relatability fosters a strong emotional connection between readers and the stories.

Kathleen Glasgow's work navigates themes of mental health, self-discovery, friendship, creativity, family, resilience, and hope. Her ability to tackle these themes with sensitivity and authenticity has made her a respected and influential voice in the world of young adult literature, resonating with readers who appreciate the depth and authenticity of her storytelling.

IMPACTS

Kathleen Glasgow's work, including novels like "Girl in Pieces," "How to Make Friends with the Dark," and "You'd Be Home Now," has left a profound impact on readers in deeply human ways:

1. **Emotional Connection**: Kathleen's writing is known for its emotional depth and authenticity. Readers often describe feeling a strong emotional connection to her characters and their journeys.

They resonate with the raw, unfiltered portrayal of complex human experiences, from pain and despair to resilience and hope.

2. **Empathy and Understanding**: Kathleen's novels explore sensitive and often stigmatized topics, such as self-harm, mental health, grief, and trauma. Her compassionate and empathetic approach to these subjects helps readers better understand the challenges faced by individuals dealing with such issues. Readers often report gaining insights that foster greater empathy for others in their own lives.

3. **Validation of Feelings**: Many readers have found validation in Kathleen's work. Her characters' struggles mirror the experiences of real people dealing with similar challenges. This validation can be immensely comforting for

readers who may have felt alone or misunderstood in their own battles with mental health or adversity.

4. **Inspiration for Resilience**: Kathleen's characters often exhibit remarkable resilience in the face of adversity. Readers find inspiration in their journeys, learning that it's possible to overcome even the darkest of circumstances. Her stories offer a glimmer of hope and the belief that healing and recovery are achievable.

5. **Encouragement for Open Conversations**: Kathleen's willingness to tackle difficult subjects head-on has encouraged readers to engage in open and honest conversations about topics like mental health, self-harm, and grief. Her work has been a catalyst for important dialogues within families, friendships, and communities.

6. **Sense of Belonging**: Kathleen's novels create a sense of belonging for readers who may have experienced similar struggles. Knowing that others have faced and triumphed over similar challenges can provide comfort and a sense of community.

7. **Impact on Young Adults**: Kathleen's young adult novels, in particular, resonate with teenagers and young adults navigating the complexities of adolescence and early adulthood. Her books provide relatable and authentic narratives that address issues relevant to this age group, helping them feel seen and understood.

In a deeply human way, Kathleen Glasgow's work touches the hearts and minds of her readers, offering solace, understanding, and a sense of shared humanity. Her ability to explore the depth of human emotions and experiences through her writing has left an indelible mark on those who have been fortunate enough to encounter her work.

CONCLUSION

Kathleen Glasgow's enduring legacy and contributions to young adult literature are a testament to the power of storytelling and the profound impact a writer can have on readers, particularly young adults.

Throughout her career, Kathleen's work has stood out for its unflinching honesty and its willingness to confront complex and often stigmatized topics. She has tackled themes like self-harm, mental health, trauma, and recovery with a rare authenticity that resonates deeply with her readers. Her novels provide a safe space for young adults to explore and process their own feelings and experiences.

One of Kathleen's most significant contributions has been her ability to create complex, relatable, and multi-dimensional characters. Her protagonists, often young women dealing with adversity, are not one-dimensional heroes but individuals with flaws, scars, and vulnerabilities. This approach has allowed readers to connect with her characters on a deeply human level, recognizing their own struggles and strengths within the stories.

Kathleen's work has also opened up meaningful conversations. Through her novels, she has encouraged discussions about mental health, self-harm, grief, and the challenges faced by young people. Her willingness to shine a light on these issues has helped break down stigmas and foster greater empathy and understanding.

Perhaps one of Kathleen's most enduring legacies is her impact on young readers. Her novels offer a lifeline to those who may be struggling, showing them that they are not alone and that healing and recovery are possible. Her stories provide a sense of hope and the belief that even in the darkest of times, there is a path toward resilience and growth.

In a genre often dismissed or overlooked, Kathleen Glasgow's work has elevated the standards for young adult literature. Her novels are a testament to the emotional depth and complexity that can be achieved in storytelling aimed at young readers. Her legacy is one of empowerment, empathy, and the belief that literature has the power to touch hearts and change lives.

Kathleen Glasgow's enduring contributions to young adult literature will continue to inspire and resonate with generations of readers, reminding them of the transformative potential of storytelling and the enduring impact of an author who fearlessly embraces the human experience.

Made in the USA
Middletown, DE
01 November 2024

63684427R00020